ESCAPING SPACE

BY LAURA LANE

The Child's World®
childsworld.com

Published by The Child's World®
1980 Lookout Drive • Mankato, MN 56003-1705
800-599-READ • www.childsworld.com

Photographs ©: JSC/NASA, cover, 1, 5, 6, 9, 20, 23, 24, 26; KSC/NASA, 11; Sputnik/Alamy, 12; AP Images, 14, 17; Shutterstock Images, 16; PSG/Newscom, 18; MSFC/NASA, 22

ISBN 9781503825314
LCCN 2017959694

Printed in the United States of America
PA02377

TABLE OF CONTENTS

FAST FACTS

- The Soviet Union, now Russia, became the first country to launch a **satellite**, *Sputnik I*, into space on October 4, 1957.
- *Sputnik*'s launch started the space race between the Soviet Union and the United States. Each country wanted to be the first to explore space.
- Soviet **cosmonaut** Yuri Gagarin became the first human in space on April 12, 1961.
- **Astronaut** Alan B. Shepard became the first American in space on May 5, 1961.
- Astronaut John Glenn became the first American to **orbit** Earth on February 20, 1962.
- On July 20, 1969, American astronauts Neil Armstrong and Buzz Aldrin were the first humans to land on the moon. They were also the first people to walk on the moon.
- There is barely any oxygen in space. Spacecrafts need to have enough oxygen for astronauts to breathe during their mission. Otherwise the astronauts would die in space.

Space is a very dangerous place. Astronauts are at risk from the moment they enter the spacecraft to the minute they land back on Earth. ▶

- There is also very little gravity in space. If astronauts went outside of a spacecraft without being attached, they would float away.
- Starting in 1998, 16 countries joined together to build the International Space Station. The space station allows people from different countries to live and work together in space.

Chapter 1

FIRE ON THE SPACE STATION MIR

What a strange place to die, thought American astronaut Jerry Linenger. The air on the Russian space station Mir was filled with smoke. Jerry couldn't breathe or see very well. He searched for an oxygen mask. Once he could breathe freely, he could find an extinguisher to put out the fire.

There wasn't much time. The fire was huge. He thought it looked like 100 sparklers all lit up on the Fourth of July. It was quickly consuming the space station. Jerry worried the fire would burn through Mir's thin aluminum **hull**. This would create a hole in the space station. If this happened, air from the space station would leak out into space. The crew on board would suffocate to death.

◀ **Jerry Linenger traveled more than 50 million miles (80 million km) when he was aboard the Mir space station.**

The space shuttle *Atlantis* had flown Jerry to Mir on January 12, 1997. Jerry came to Mir for a five-month stay. He joined Valery Korzun, a Russian cosmonaut and Mir's commander. Sasha Kaleri, another Russian cosmonaut, was also on board.

THE MIGHTY MIR

The space station was more magnificent than Jerry imagined it would be. It was large and impressive. From the outside, it looked like six school buses joined together. The station had several different **modules**. On the inside, however, the space station was cluttered. Old equipment, tools, cables, water tanks, and floating garbage bags were scattered around the modules.

In February, two other Russian cosmonauts, Vasily Tsibliev and Sasha Lazutkin, and a German researcher, Reinhold Ewald, arrived at Mir. Late one night, Sasha twisted a dial to turn on an oxygen canister. He breathed in the oxygen and could feel the warm air flow out. Sasha thought everything was working normally.

Suddenly, a strange hissing sound caught his attention. Sasha turned around and saw a flame shoot out from the oxygen canister. Valery sprang into action.

▲ **The first Mir space station was launched in February 1986.**

He told the crew to put on oxygen masks. He ordered Sasha to power up one of the space capsules. They were docked on Mir in case the crew needed to escape. The astronauts and cosmonauts had trained for years to learn how to handle dangerous events in space.

Jerry searched for an oxygen mask quickly. The smoke was so thick he could barely see anything. Finally, Jerry found a mask.

He yanked it off the wall and pulled it over his head. He flipped the lever to turn the oxygen on. Nothing happened. Jerry breathed in, but there was no oxygen coming out of the canister. He breathed in again, and the mask collapsed around his face. The oxygen mask had failed.

Jerry quickly began searching for another mask. As he was searching, he thought of his family back on Earth. He wanted to be sure that he would see them again. Finally, he found a second mask. He pulled it over his head, flipped the lever, and oxygen filled his mask. He could breathe freely again.

Jerry handed fire extinguishers to Valery. It took several extinguishers to put out the fire. However, even though the fire had been put out, the crew was still in great danger. The only things keeping the crew alive were the oxygen masks. The space station was filled with smoke. The air was not breathable. The crew hoped the air filters could clean the air before their masks ran out of oxygen.

Valery's oxygen ran out first. He took off his mask and sniffed. He was able to breathe. The space station's filters had done their job. The filters cleared the smoke out, so the crew could breathe again. The crew had survived the deadly fire on Mir.

In case of a fire on a spacecraft, astronauts and cosmonauts ▶ have masks that will protect their lungs from being damaged by smoke.

ROMINGER
PAYETTE
JERNIGAN
BARRY

Chapter 2

THE FIRST SPACEWALKER'S NEAR DISASTER

On March 18, 1965, Russian cosmonaut Alexei Leonov was preparing to do something no one had ever done before. He was about to become the first person ever to walk in space.

On that day, Alexei and Pavel Belyayev, also a cosmonaut, launched into space aboard the *Voskhod-2* spacecraft. The purpose of their mission was to discover if a person could survive in a space suit in open space. When they reached orbit, Pavel opened the outer air lock. Alexei stepped inside. The air lock was like a tunnel attached to the spaceship. The outer **hatch** at the end of the air lock opened. Alexei pushed himself into space.

Alexei was attached to the *Voskhod-2* by a 16-foot (5 m) cord. This cord kept him from drifting off into space.

◄ **Alexei Leonov was a pioneer for floating free in space, which is also called "extravehicular activity," or EVA.**

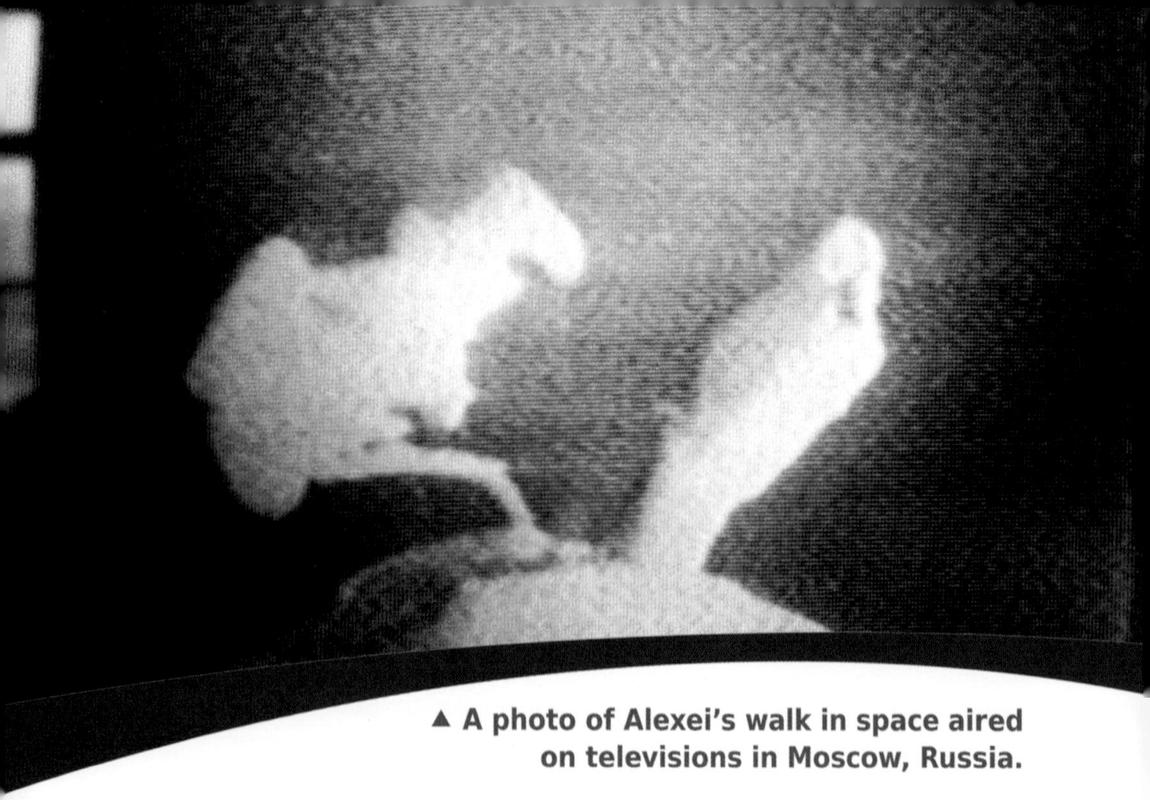

▲ **A photo of Alexei's walk in space aired on televisions in Moscow, Russia.**

Alexei had been walking in space for just ten minutes. Then Pavel told him it was time to come back inside. Alexei headed for the air lock. He tried to fit in, but he realized something was wrong. His space suit had inflated like a balloon. The suit was too big to fit inside the opening of the air lock.

Alexei opened a valve and let out some of the oxygen in his space suit. He risked losing all of his oxygen. If he could not get back inside the air lock, he would die in space.

With less air in his space suit, Alexei could fit inside the air lock. He used his arms to pull himself in and closed the hatch. This took nearly all his strength. He had little oxygen left. It was hard to breathe. Alexei was drenched in sweat.

Alexei finally made it safely back inside the *Voskhod-2*. Then he discovered another serious problem. The oxygen controls inside the spacecraft were malfunctioning. The levels were rising too quickly. High oxygen levels made the spacecraft **flammable**. A spark from the engines on the spacecraft could cause a massive explosion. Fortunately, nothing sparked.

Alexei and Pavel were safe. They steered *Voskhod-2* back to Earth, thankful they had made it through their mission. But they quickly realized something else was wrong. *Voskhod-2* couldn't make it back to Earth. Its automatic system to reenter Earth's atmosphere had failed.

Alexei and Pavel realized their only option was to guide their spaceship back to Earth **manually**. No one had ever done this before. Alexei and Pavel had to position the *Voskhod-2* at the perfect angle to reenter Earth's atmosphere. If they made a mistake, the spacecraft could explode. They both would die.

The cosmonauts carefully directed the *Voskhod-2*. The ship began spinning. Everything became dark inside the spacecraft. Alexei worried they were dropping down into a deep canyon on Earth. They had no control over the landing. The spaceship was dropping faster and faster.

The spaceship crashed to the ground with a big thump. Alexei and Pavel tumbled around inside. Finally, they slid to a halt.

They had landed in the Northern Ural Mountains in Russia. The forest was thick with trees, and snow covered the ground.

The cosmonauts had extensive survival training. They set up their emergency radio and broadcast their signal in Morse code.

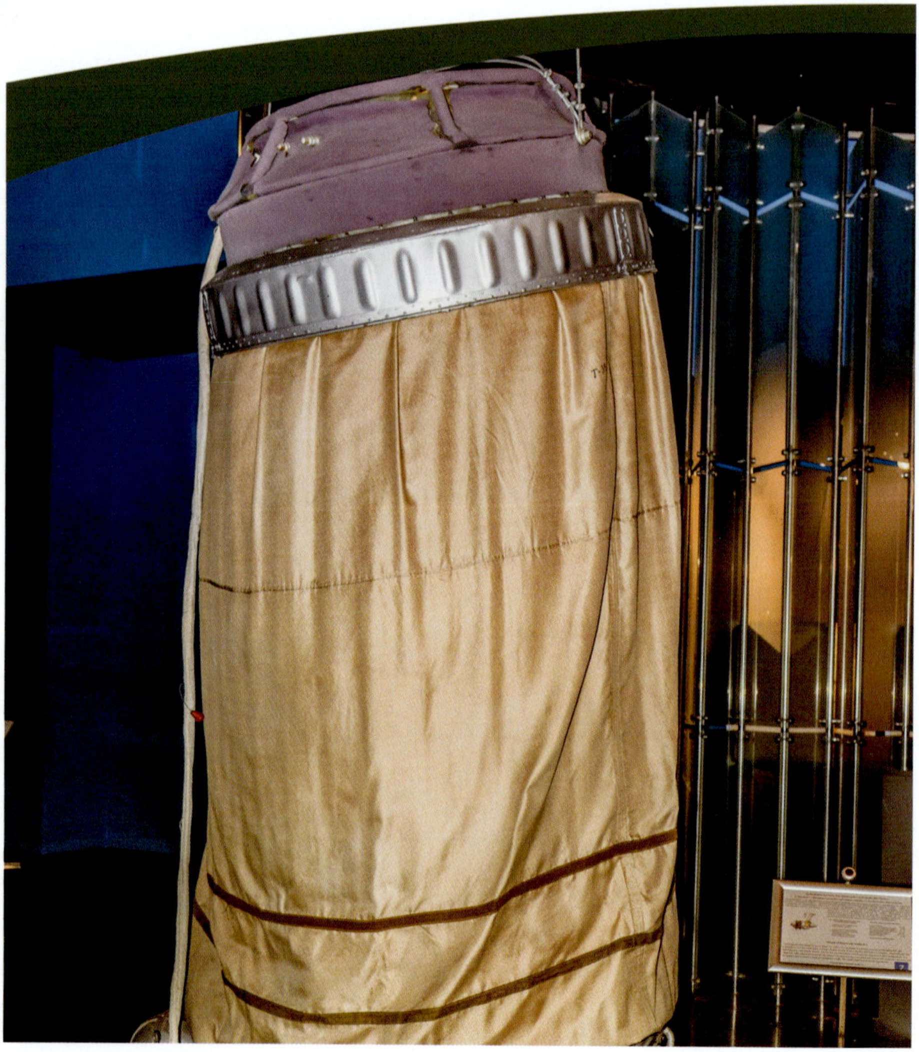

▲ **The Space Museum in Moscow has the air lock from the *Voskhod-2* on display.**

▲ **Alexei and Pavel were welcomed as heroes when they returned to Moscow on March 23, 1965.**

It would be a while before anyone could reach them that high up in the mountains. As night fell, the temperature dropped below –22 degrees Fahrenheit (–30°C). They had no heat in the spaceship. After their risky journey back from space, Alexei and Pavel could freeze to death overnight on Earth.

Hours passed. As the sun came up, the cosmonauts realized they had made it through the night. A rescue party arrived on skis. After another night in the woods, Alexei and Pavel skied to safety with their rescue team. Later a helicopter came to pick them up. They were finally safe.

Chapter 3

APOLLO 13'S DANGEROUS MISSION

American astronaut Jack Swigert spoke calmly. "Houston, we've had a problem here." **Mission Control** listened to his plea for help on the other end. It was April 13, 1970. Two days earlier, Jack and his crewmates, astronauts Jim Lovell and Fred Haise, had launched into space. Their mission was called Apollo 13. They were headed to the moon.

It was a complicated mission. The *Apollo* spacecraft was made up of three parts. There was the Command Module, the Service Module, and the Lunar Module. The Command Module was called *Odyssey*. The crew lived in *Odyssey* as they flew to the moon. The Service Module contained the fuel, oxygen, and rocket engine. The Lunar Module was called *Aquarius*. It had a very small area designed for two astronauts and a pair of tiny instrument panels.

◄ **Jack Swigert (center) was not originally part of Apollo 13. He joined Jim Lovell (left) and Fred Haise (right) on the mission.**

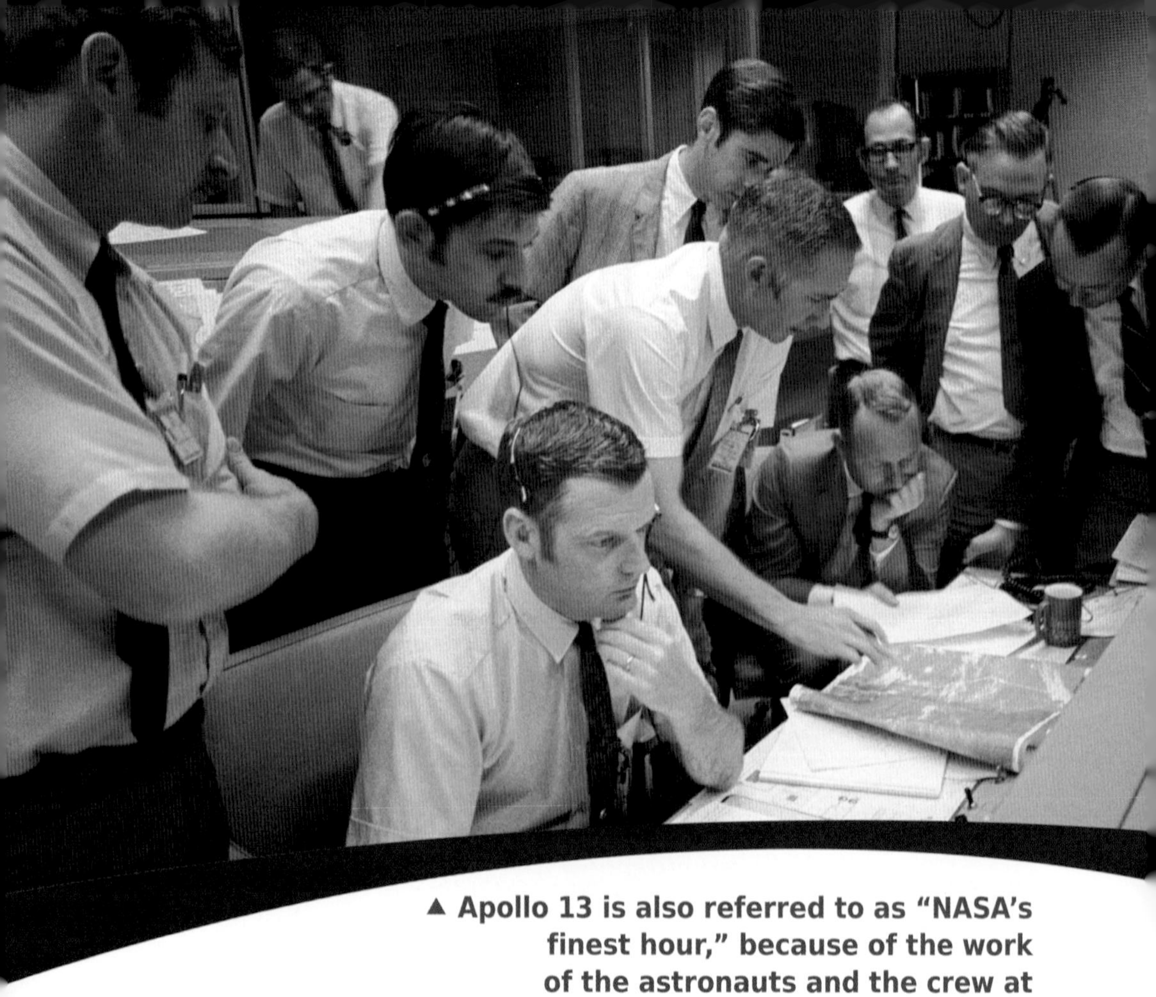

▲ **Apollo 13 is also referred to as "NASA's finest hour," because of the work of the astronauts and the crew at Mission Control.**

When the crew got close to the moon, Jim and Fred were supposed to separate *Aquarius* from the spacecraft. Then they needed to land *Aquarius* on the moon's surface. Jim and Fred would then collect samples of moon rock to bring back to Earth. They were also supposed to set up instruments to study the moon's surface.

But something went terribly wrong. At 9:07 p.m. on April 13, the crew heard a loud bang. *Odyssey* began shaking.

An oxygen tank had exploded. *Odyssey* began losing breathable air and power. The astronauts would not survive for very long.

Jim looked at Fred and saw his eyes widen in fear. The three astronauts were scared. They thought a meteor had hit their ship.

Mission Control knew the astronauts were in grave danger. The flight controllers quickly scanned their monitors. They examined data to find out what had gone wrong with the ship. The sole focus became getting the crew back to Earth safely. Thousands of people at Mission Control began working around the clock to figure out how to get the astronauts home.

Mission Control instructed the crew to go inside *Aquarius* until the spacecraft got closer to Earth. *Aquarius* was only designed to support two men for two days. It would take four days to get back to Earth. Jim did not panic. Fred was trained to fly *Aquarius*. Jim hoped Fred and Mission Control could figure out ways to make *Aquarius*'s resources last longer.

The crew turned off as many systems as they could to save power. There was no heat. Temperatures in *Aquarius* dropped down to near freezing. The astronauts carefully measured out water so they would not run out. The conditions were cold, cramped, and uncomfortable. At one point Fred developed a fever and began shaking violently.

After four long days, the spacecraft reached Earth again. *Odyssey* was the part of the spacecraft designed to reenter Earth's atmosphere. The crew went back into *Odyssey* and prepared for landing. All three of the astronauts tightened their shoulder belts and lap belts.

APOLLO SPACECRAFT

The design of the *Apollo* spaceship, including all of the modules used by the Apollo 13 crew.

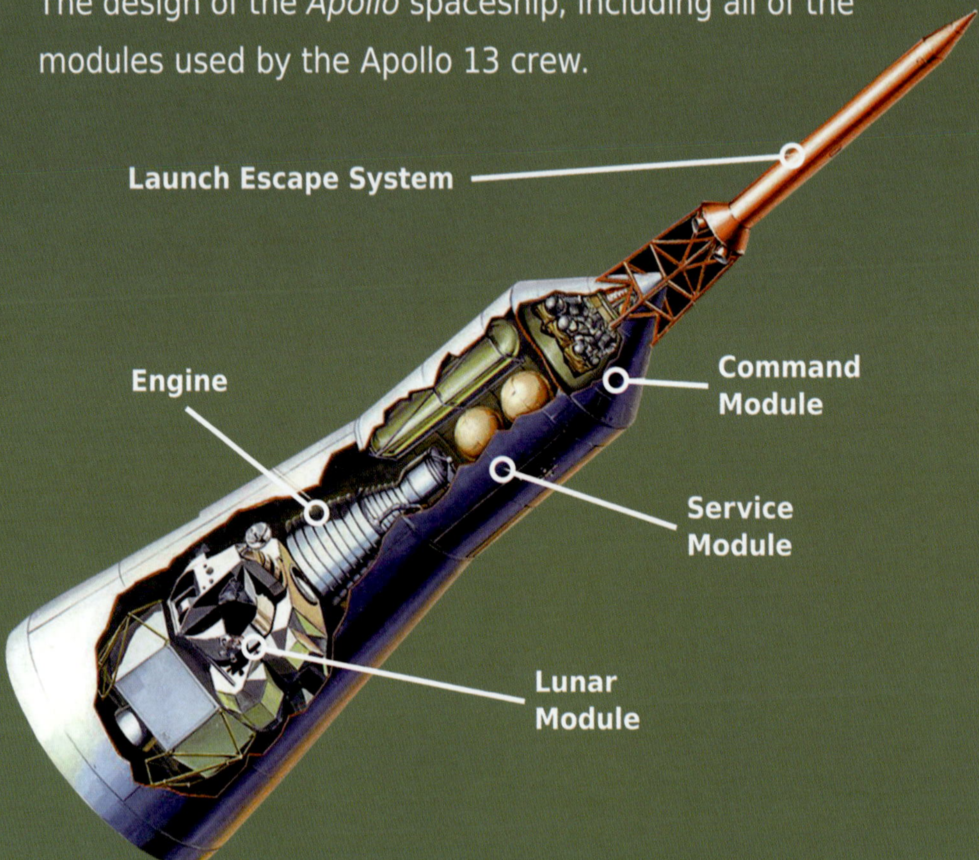

On April 17, *Odyssey* splashed down in the Pacific Ocean. The astronauts were rescued from the ocean. They were taken onto the U.S.S. *Iwo Jima*. The astronauts never lost hope that they would get home safely. Failure was never an option.

▲ ***Odyssey* landed approximately 4 miles (6 km) away from the *Iwo Jima*.**

United States

Chapter 4

A SECRET MISSION GONE WRONG

It was December 2, 1988. American astronaut Mike Mullane was strapped into his seat on the space shuttle *Atlantis*. He was waiting patiently for the ship to launch. But bad weather was delaying the takeoff into space.

Mike and the other astronauts aboard *Atlantis* were on a top-secret mission. They were flying into space to set up a spy satellite. The satellite used radar, a device that locates other objects, to see images through the clouds. It was designed to spy on Soviet forces in Europe.

Mike thought the launch was one of the most dangerous parts of space travel. He prayed for a safe flight. Finally, *Atlantis* blasted into the sky and entered into orbit. Mike felt relieved the launch had gone smoothly. Once in space, the crew got to work.

◀ ***Atlantis* launched from the Kennedy Space Center in Cape Canaveral, Florida.**

▲ **Mike Mullane (top right) was on board *Atlantis* with four other crew members.**

The shuttle had a robotic arm attached to it. Mike used the arm to carefully guide and release the satellite into space. It was successful.

The next morning, Mission Control called. They asked if the astronauts had seen anything fly by the shuttle windows during the launch. None of the crew had seen anything unusual.

Photographs taken during the launch, however, told a different story. It looked as if the tip of the nose cone on the right rocket booster had broken off. It had hit tiles on the outside of the shuttle. Mike used the robotic arm to take another look at the tiles. The crew thought many of the tiles appeared damaged.

Damaged tiles were a big problem. The tiles acted as a heat shield. When a spacecraft reenters Earth's atmosphere, its temperature heats up. The tiles on the shuttle prevent the heat from melting a hole in it. If the tiles were damaged, the astronauts might die when they returned to Earth.

Atlantis commander Robert "Hoot" Gibson thought the tiles were badly damaged. Mission Control disagreed. They said the tiles were not damaged enough to pose a risk to the crew's safety. The astronauts looked at each other in disbelief. They could not believe what they were hearing. Hoot was frustrated and angry. Mike worried that Mission Control knew the shuttle had suffered serious damage, but that they were hiding that fact from the crew. Even if the tiles were damaged, the astronauts had no way to repair them.

HOW DID THE CREW OF *ATLANTIS* SURVIVE?

The damaged area on the outside of the space shuttle was the one place that had two layers of metal. The double layer of steel and aluminum provided extra protection. It gave the shuttle enough time to reenter Earth's atmosphere before the heat melted a hole in the shuttle. "The damage had been sustained in the only place where it could exist and still be survivable," Mike later remembered. The astronauts felt very lucky to have survived the mission.

The *Atlantis* crew had no choice but to return to Earth. As they prepared to reenter Earth's atmosphere, Hoot thought they were all going to die. He thought *Atlantis* would not sustain the heat of Earth's atmosphere. The space shuttle, and the crew, could be destroyed. The crew started their mission back to Earth, unsure of their fate.

The crew was worried and scared. The return home seemed to take forever. They were about to reenter Earth's atmosphere. The crew members were relieved when the shuttle safely reentered the atmosphere. They landed safely. The heat shield had worked.

Then the astronauts got out of the shuttle. They were stunned at what they saw. More than 700 tiles on *Atlantis* had been damaged. It was the greatest heat shield damage the astronauts had ever seen. It was a miracle they had all survived.

THINK ABOUT IT

- What types of things can go wrong during space travel?
- What surprised you about the types of dangers the astronauts faced?
- Knowing the risks, why would someone want to become an astronaut? Are there positive things about astronauts' jobs?
- Would you want to become an astronaut when you grow up? Why or why not?

GLOSSARY

astronaut (AS-truh-not): An astronaut is a person who travels in a spacecraft to outer space. Astronaut Alan B. Shepard was the first American in space.

cosmonaut (KAHZ-muh-not): A cosmonaut is a Russian astronaut. Cosmonaut Yuri Gagarin was the first person in space.

flammable (FLAM-uh-bull): Something is flammable when it easily catches on fire. High oxygen levels made the spaceship flammable.

hatch (HACH): A hatch is a small opening or door. Alexei opened the hatch of the spaceship and stepped into the air lock.

hull (HULL): The hull is the main body of a spacecraft. Jerry worried the fire would burn a hole in the space station's aluminum hull.

manually (MAN-u-al-ee): To operate something manually means to operate it by hand. Alexei and Pavel had to fly their spaceship back to Earth manually.

Mission Control (MISH-un kun-TROLL): Mission Control is a facility where people oversee the flight of a spacecraft and communicate with the astronauts. Jack told Mission Control there was a huge problem when *Odyssey* began losing oxygen and power.

modules (MOD-jewls): Modules are a group of parts or units. The space station Mir had several different modules.

orbit (OR-bit): To orbit is to move in a curved path around a star, planet, or moon. The space shuttle *Atlantis* launched into the sky and entered into orbit around Earth.

satellite (SAT-uh-lite): A satellite is a man-made object placed in space to gather information or for communication. Russia was the first country to launch a satellite into space.

TO LEARN MORE

Books

DeCristofano, Carolyn. *Ultimate Space Atlas: Maps, Games, Activities and More for Hours of Galactic Fun!* Washington, DC: National Geographic, 2017.

Kespert, Deborah, and David Baker. *Space Academy: How to Fly Spacecraft Step by Step.* New York, NY: Thames & Hudson, 2013.

Newland, Sonya. *Space Exploration: Triumphs and Tragedies.* New York, NY: Crabtree Publishing, 2016.

Web Sites

Visit our Web site for links about escaping space:
childsworld.com/links

Note to Parents, Teachers, and Librarians: We routinely verify our Web links to make sure they are safe and active sites. So encourage your readers to check them out!

SELECTED BIBLIOGRAPHY

Linenger, Jerry M. *Off the Planet: Surviving Five Perilous Months aboard the Space Station Mir.* New York, NY: McGraw-Hill, 2000. Print.

McKinnon, Mika. "50 Years Ago, the First Spacewalk Nearly Ended in Tragedy." *Gizmodo.* Gizmodo Media Group, 18 Mar. 2015. Web. 12 Oct. 2017.

Scott, David, and Alexei Leonov. *Two Sides of the Moon.* New York, NY: St. Martin's Press, 2004. Print.

INDEX

ABOUT THE AUTHOR

Laura Lane lives in Wisconsin with her husband and two children. She enjoys writing about science and social studies for children.